SOCIAL CONFIDENCE

HOW TO BOOST YOUR SOCIAL CONFIDENCE AND SUCCEED IN ALL SOCIAL SITUATIONS

Copyright ©
David C. Allen 2017
All Rights Reserved.

Table of Contents

Introduction 6

What Is Social Confidence? 10

The Art of the Smile 16

Listening 25

Rapport 40

Inside Out 59

Why Do People Fear Social Interactions? 67

Ego vs. Self-Esteem 75

Get Out Of Your (Un)Sociable Comfort Zone 84

Don't Overdo It 90

Reading Other People 116

Dealing with Rejection 127

Conclusion 138

Introduction

You may have a friend or know someone who shines with social confidence. This could be a co-worker that seems to know everyone in the office. This may be a friend that gets invited to all the parties and makes all the connections. This could be a sales agent you work with that always closes the deals and makes great clients.

Whatever form or occupation these people might have, you can bet your bottom dollar that they have mastered the art of getting along with other people. Anyone who is comfortable with other people radiates a certain glow from within themselves. It's got nothing to do with their skin but is more likely an energy that comes from their social confidence.

What do you say to yourself about your social life and social abilities? How do you feel about socializing, about being around others? Do you feel anxious, tense, stuck, frustrated, discouraged, or hopeless? Do you feel like you've tried everything and nothing works?

And yet you are reading this book. Perhaps there is a sliver of hope left. Perhaps you have not tried everything. What if it were possible for you to shift something inside of yourself so that you could have better conversations with people you just met? Better yet, what if you could actually enjoy those conversations? What if you shifted something in yourself so you did not feel that nervous about meeting someone new? What if you were not really worried about whether they were going to like you? How would you behave? What would you say or do?

The truth is, it is possible to feel relaxed and curious when meeting new people, to feel nervous yet excited before flirting with someone, and to feel elated after making friends or going on a date. The anxiety and fear you feel around others is the result of a learned pattern. It is a pattern of specific thoughts, feelings, and behaviors—all of which you have the power to change.

This book will provide you with the right tools and exercises you need to start to make that shift. You will learn exactly what thoughts, feelings, and actions are tripping you up and learn just what to do to set yourself on a course towards greater social confidence.

After learning all the material in this book, and doing the exercises, I am confident that you will be able to overcome crippling shyness and lack of social confidence to create satisfying friendships, enjoy rich and fulfilling relationships, and pursue the career and life goals that are most meaningful to you. No matter how long you have struggled with shyness, or how severe your social anxiety, it is possible for you to take action that will help you improve.

Even if that seems like an unbelievable stretch to you now, I encourage you to keep reading. You do not have to believe it yet. All I am asking is that you remain open to the possibility that your life can be different. To hold it as possible that you can learn new ideas, new skills, and new approaches that will shift your experience and help you get more of what you want out of life.

What Is Social Confidence?

You may have already defined this term on your own in efforts to give meaning to your own lack of skills. But it's not just important to define what social confidence is. Learning where it comes from and what causes it to appear will greatly improve your ability to deal with other people.

Social confidence is the knowledge that you won't make a fool of yourself when you're with other people. It's the fact lying at the back of your head that lets you know that when you're with other people, you'll be able to relate to them and get on their good side without trouble.

That is the goal of this book, to help you achieve social confidence. You won't be afraid of being with other people and you'll know that wherever you are, you'll be comfortable and accepted. You won't be shying away from parties or simple lunch gatherings at the office and when you're better at being with other people, other people will find it more comfortable to be around you as well.

Why Do I Need Social Confidence?

You may already be happy with the level of social confidence that you have. You probably already have a small group of friends that you're happy being around. That's fine, but you could be achieving more with a higher level of social confidence.

You get more opportunities – Why? Because you get to meet more people. When you radiate social confidence, you're not just drawn to people; people are also drawn to you. You never know who you could be attracting. It could be a fashion agent or a potential employer or your next love story. It's all just waiting to happen!

You learn new things – There's no telling who gets into your circle or network next. The more you're happy being with other people, the more you appreciate how diverse they can be. Every new friend is a new set of stories, experiences, and valuable information you can learn.

You become more comfortable in your own skin – Although counting your friends and networks may not be a good idea, knowing there are people happy to have you around makes you more comfortable being yourself. You become less afraid to do the things you want because you have people that are willing to support your decisions.

You discover more about yourself – When you open your doors to other people, you don't just learn about them. You also learn things about yourself. Humans have a habit of seeing themselves in other people, especially when there is much in common between them. You don't necessarily lose yourself in your circle of friends; that's usually where you find most of yourself.

What Comprises Social Confidence?

To attain social confidence, you need to understand where it comes from. When you see a stranger sitting at a coffee shop that has garnered your interest, do you just stare at them from afar or consider the possibility of making a new friend?

When someone approaches you at a party and strikes up a conversation with you, are you more inclined to shy away and go to a different area of the party or do you engage with this person and learn something new?

Social confidence is the ability to move towards the decision that will earn you a new interaction. It's the ability to be able to choose to be with people in which you don't compromise yourself. Interestingly, it stems from the combination of a few learnable concepts.

Empathy

Rapport

Listening

Discipline

Smiling

They may not be intimidating skills to learn, but individually they can stump almost anyone. The succeeding chapters of this book will handle each of these skills individually, with each chapter making you an expert.

The Art of the Smile

You may be surprised to know that something as simple as smiling would lead to increased social confidence but take a good look at yourself and how you behave around other people.

Do you smile a lot? If you do, what are the things that make you smile? Are they other people or things made by other people?

The very definition of the word smile pertains to a grin that acts as a result of something happy or amusing. There is a deeper definition to that. To get to that definition, you should ask yourself a personal question:

Are You Happy Around Other People?

To be socially confident, you should enjoy being around other people. When that happens, all the other skills you're going to learn in this book will fall out naturally.

If your presence around other people is forced and your smile is artificial, other people will notice that and in turn, they will have their own reservations about being around you. So, it's not just a smile. It's a signal that says you're happy being around other people.

What If I'm not Happy Around Others?

There could be a few reasons behind that. You could be anxious about being with other people. You could be afraid of embarrassing yourself. You could also be attracted to who you're with, causing a change in behavior. Worse, you could have trust issues with other people, causing you to attach social interaction with a bad connotation.

One painful truth you will learn about social confidence is that you should like it. There are no shortcuts or loopholes here. Being with people should be something you enjoy.

With all that you stand to gain from building social confidence, you have more than enough reason to smile when you meet someone new!

For the Socially Anxious

Despite those reasons, some people are clinically proven to be awkward when it comes to social gatherings. These are people who experience social anxiety.

For these people, social interaction works like an allergen that triggers unpleasant sensations within them. Their stomachs churn, they go pale, they get dizzy and have all sorts of other discomforts at the mere mention of the idea of seeing people. It's not that they don't like socializing. Their perceptions have already programmed their bodies to respond negatively to the idea.

"Treatments"

But just like allergic attacks, there are still ways to relieve these symptoms to bring yourself closer to becoming more socially confident.

One of the first things you'll have to do, interestingly, is to expose yourself to your allergen in controlled amounts. Yes, that means tackling the problem head on. Many experts point towards taking baby steps with social interactions. Talk with someone on the phone. Sit down for a cup of coffee with someone.

It doesn't even have to be someone new. It can be someone you've known for a long time. It could also be a family member you trust deeply.

Setting up a gradual plan, you dive deeper into social activity. Ensuring that the next activity has more exposure than the last, you train your body to tolerate the activity, just like the way it would tolerate an allergen when treated with the same process.

You could start with a cup of coffee with your siblings which could be followed by a cup of coffee with strangers and one of your relatives the next day. If that goes well, it could be followed by a cup of coffee shared between you and someone new.

The idea is to control the amounts of exposure you get until you reach the point that it's no longer an issue for you and your body.

And when your body becomes comfortable being around other people, you wouldn't find it hard to smile anymore.

The Importance of a Smile

Still don't think smiles are important? The words of experts may not sway you, but what about the opinions of the public, to which you want to appeal?

More than 70% of American adults believe that a bad smile will ruin your career.

More than 80% of the same population said that they will remember someone with a great smile.

A whopping 99% of people in the United States say that a smile is a person's best asset.

Take note that these aren't the opinions of experts. These are opinions of the public. These are regular people you might meet on the street, at work and even on the way home. We are all programmed to like someone based on their smile. The numbers don't lie.

How to Smile – The Brush Technique

So, you get the idea; you need to smile. But a fake smile is just as bad as not smiling at all. You'll be surprised to know that there are some techniques people have used to improve their smiles that don't just involve brushing your teeth every night.

Provided that your dental care routine is sound, you can boost the attractiveness of your smile with a simple trick. Take note, this trick has been used by professional models and cameramen when dealing with their subjects. It's known as the "brush" technique.

Aptly named, this method of smiling will give you the best angle and formation of your grin to show a sincere and comfortable smile. All you need to do is to say the word "brush". You can try it right now. Say it.

Didn't that force a grin on your face? Did you feel the corners of your lips pushing into your cheekbones? That's a sign that you've done it right! Instead of saying "cheese", use the brush instead and you'll find more people becoming attracted to your smile!

Not fond of brushes? That's not a problem! You can also try the word "eight". It does the same thing to your jaw and lips.

These two simple words will change the way you smile and turn every grin into a photo op with the people around you! And your journey to social confidence only begins at this point!

Listening

If you've read the first two chapters before this one, you've already exhibited enough skill to listen. It takes serious dedication to channel your attention and focus onto someone that isn't yourself.

Sure, your problems and perceptions are the most important things to you, but what about the perceptions and stories of those around you? To gain social confidence, you need to learn to give more than to receive. The good thing about this is that the rewards outweigh the efforts.

Listening Defined

Take note that you can hear something and not listen to it. These two things are completely different. Hearing something means your auditory faculties are recognizing the presence of stimuli, nothing more. When you listen, you don't just hear. You internalize and understand.

It's so easy to listen to yourself. You think you're the best person to listen to; because who understands yourself better than you? But what about other people? Sure, you've listened to class and your peers and your family. How about a stranger?

What if someone starts talking to you? What if it begins as a casual conversation that has the potential to become a meaningful social activity? Are you ready to listen to it?

If someone told you that within the things they say, there is a reward or a cash prize waiting for you. You would probably remember everything that would be said to you. This is because you perceive an inherent advantage that will come out of listening.

What if there weren't any promises like that when you listen to someone? Would you still feel inclined to listen? Sure, you listen to things from time to time. These could be the things that already interest you; things that matter to you. But what if no such establishment has been made in the first place? Are you willing to invest your time and mental effort into listening to someone?

As mentioned in the earlier chapters, listening should stem from a natural desire to learn more about someone. You're going to have to be interested in someone to be able to listen to them.

Their words may not hold much value at the start, but stick around and you might just walk away with something valuable.

Effective Listening Made Easy

At the center of it all, the capacity to precisely intercept and process input from a source is represented by proper listening. In your case, you're the listener and your sources are the people around you.

When you're up and about, do you keep yourself to yourself? Do you pump an introvert bubble and stay inside the whole time? You may not notice this, but that bubble is very visible at certain times, especially to the people around you. This bubble sometimes comes off as an unwillingness to listen. This could, in turn, drive people away from you.

What could this bubble be? It could be a pair of earphones permanently glued to the sides of your head. It could be that book you never seem to finish in the subway. It could also be that glass of wine that you could never seem to finish at a party. These things could give off the impression that you don't want to be disturbed, despite being in a social setting!

Eye Contact

There's something about what you look at that says so much about your current temperament. You may need your ears for listening but your eyes can give off the wrong impression if you don't know where to place them!

In some cultures, not looking at the person you're talking to is considered as extremely rude. Even if your ears are receiving what someone else is saying, you won't look like you're listening if you're not looking at who you're with.

It's important to maintain eye contact. It doesn't just show you're interested, it also shows you're sincere about the conversation. Any extrovert will immediately know you're disinterested when you bury yourself in your phone, book or even your beer.

The Two Second Rule

Listening isn't just about nodding and agreeing with someone when they're telling you something. It's a delicate balance of responding and receiving messages. This is where the two-second rule comes in.

Don't you hate it if someone would interrupt you in the middle of a story with something irrelevant? You could be giving off the same impression when you're with other people. You may just think you're participating in a conversation, but you may also be interrupting someone's story the moment you open your mouth.

That is why you should wait at least two seconds when someone is finished speaking. Those two seconds are to give them enough time to follow up what they are saying. It also gives you enough time to absorb what they've said. It's a great tool to fit in with others. You'll be more respectful and other people will find it easy talking to you.

Mirroring

What the FBI considers as one of the best skills of a con-man, you can also use to make heads turn towards you.

One of the simplest ways you can engage someone is to simply match what they bring to the table in terms of your non-verbal body language.

Take some good news, for instance. When the person you're talking to is sharing some good news with you, reciprocate their smiles with a smile of your own. Follow what they're saying and determine how they're feeling. Are they excited? A hint of energy in your responses will go a long way with them.

Are they a little bit morose? Slowing down and diminishing your energy will show respect to the sad news. Hearing some nasty gossip? Sharing the emotions being projected upon you is a great way to let someone feel that you're genuinely interested in what they're saying. They'll find more confidence in you and prefer to tell you more things over time.

Take note that mirroring is different from parroting, which is twice as annoying as not listening. You don't have to repeat everything that's been said to you. That just makes you sound sarcastic.

Keeping an Open Mind

It's not just your actions and responses that need checking when you're with someone. In other cases, you also need to watch your thoughts. You may not notice it, but you could be doing all sorts of nasty things in your head while listening to someone.

First off, you could be judging someone as they speak. You could be looking at their clothes, their accessories and whatever it is they're holding. This leads you away from what they're saying. Your roaming eyes will also give the impression that you're judging them, making them feel uncomfortable around you.

Second, you could be contradicting what they say. Sure, you may be listening to what they're saying but you're already coming up with things to contradict them. You could be busy feeling hurt and agitated by something they said.

This could happen if you don't keep an open mind. Most of the time, we usually take in what people say and match them up to our own beliefs and perceptions. When something doesn't match, that's when we start treating the new information as a threat to your well-being.

Take note that you're not engaged in a debate and you're not in a courtroom. No one is under attack. The worst thing that could happen (and should happen) is that you both agree to disagree. Closing your thoughts to new information is just like closing your window to making new friends.

Don't worry, you're not supposed to stop judging what other people say. At the end of the day, what you believe in heavily depends on how you perceive what other people say. What's important is to delay your judgment about what you hear until you've heard the whole story and it's your time to think and talk. You can save yourself a lot of trouble and friendships if you're capable of just sitting and listening despite hearing something with which you don't agree.

Mental Imagery

Yes, the words are coming in and they make sense. You can see their point, but is that all you see? You can take your listening to the next level by using mental imagery.

As someone speaks to you, try to paint a mental picture of what they're saying. Don't just digest the information. Try to represent the information in your mind. You'll be surprised to know that people learn better through pictures than with words. Use this fact to your advantage.

When you're able to picture the things that you learn, you'll appreciate them better and you'll become even better at relaying information to other people. Don't just laugh at someone's story about spilling ketchup on their white shirt. Imagine what it looks like and you'll love the story even more. This won't just improve your listening skills, it will also give you a more active imagination; something that attracts a lot of people.

Relay/Feedback

This is probably the most important thing you can do as a listener. On top of nodding your head and mirroring the emotions of the speaker, you can do more by showing them that you've completely understood them.

You can do this by using conformational responses that verify your understanding. Take, for instance, a simple story about your friend going to the beach and getting a tan that turned into a nasty sunburn.

Instead of nodding your head, tell your friend you understand how that feels by using an appropriate response:

"That must be painful."

"How long were you under?"

"The doctor should have given you something for that."

These statements, although simple, allow your friend to continue their story and provide you with more details. When you have more details, it's easier to paint a mental image of their story, allowing you to appreciate what they're telling you.

By throwing out these relay statements and follow-up questions, you're not just engaging the person you're with, you're also showing them that their input is of interest to you. And you haven't even told them that they're interesting.

This will, in turn, make people more willing to share things with you because they get positive feedback from you. They know that their time spent talking to you isn't a waste because you've shown how interested you are.

Rapport

Mostly used as an important customer service concept, rapport doesn't just have a place on a floor full of telephones. At the very core, rapport could be the very thing that will allow you to become likable and approachable.

The dictionary defines rapport as the establishment of a positive relationship with someone at the beginning of an encounter. This doesn't just apply to strangers. Even long-time friends establish rapport with each other; just in a more informal manner.

Positive Relationships

No, you're not supposed to fall in love with the person you're with (unless you want to), but you're supposed to set the mood for a good conversation. That may sound like it's easier said than done, but some of the most charming people make it look so easy.

Do you have a friend that's a master of rapport? You may have picked up this book because of that friend. They just exude confidence and make people instantly want to be with them. This isn't just because of their physical appearance. These people make it easy for others to feel comfortable around them. This chapter will teach you exactly how to do that.

Breaking the Ice

Whenever meeting someone for the first time, there's always that challenge of initiating comfortable conversations. You know nothing about this person. This person knows nothing about you as well. You don't want to offend each other but could stand to win a new friend if you play your cards right. This is where an effective ice breaker comes in.

Just as the name implies, an ice breaker is supposed to "break" the invisible "stranger barrier" between you and a potential friend. This will give the two of you a reason to start communicating and building a positive relationship.

In fact, ice breakers don't just work for one-on-one encounters. They also work for larger crowds such as parties and trade shows.

Jokes

One of the best ways to break the ice is through some good old humor. Being able to find something funny in an otherwise ordinary situation is a sign of wit and charm. You will learn in the later chapters that these qualities make for great social confidence.

Everyone is given gifts; some people just don't open their packages.

Those are some nice shoes. Do they sell men's sizes where you got them?

A light joke will ease any tensions you and your target might have before talking to each other. It's even better when you're the one that initiates the humor. This displays confidence and a desire to make new friends.

Of course, you don't want to go too far with your jokes. Poking fun at religion and other people could send the wrong message and work against you. Try watching some stand-up comedians such as Kevin Hart and Chris Rock to get some good material.

Stories

At their very cores, introverts know themselves so well. This is because they allow plenty of time inspecting themselves. They're very much self-aware and can easily internalize experiences and turn them into great stories. It's just too bad they have anxiety regarding the company of other people.

If you're an introvert, there's a good chance that you're a great storyteller. Big PR and marketing companies pay top dollar for their campaigns that rely heavily on storytelling principles. Try to look back at some of the most successful commercial campaigns you've seen in the media. They mostly have one thing in common.

Many Nike commercials focus on the stories of successful athletes that have risen to the occasion. Most medical information campaigns share stories of people that have defeated debilitating conditions such as cancer. Even some fast food chains tell short-stories the evoke feelings of need in their audiences. All these campaigns used stories to elicit positive feelings from other people.

This is because stories are a good way to get people's attention. If you've got a good experience, there's a good chance you're going to turn a lot of heads when you start talking. You can prove that point to yourself. As an introvert, you're probably drawn to good stories; but that's not a fondness that introverts convey.

Check your social media feeds. Aren't they full of stories that are waiting for your attention? Aren't your feeds designed to give you stories that matter to you on a regular basis?

On top of that, storytelling is one of the best ways to see the good side of people. By listening to you, people will start making their initial perceptions about the kind of person you are. If they like your story, it's safe to assume that they like you as well. It's as simple as that.

The problem here is working on your delivery and your anxiety. Some introverts dread having to tell stories to a group of people, no matter how small. This is because they still consider it as part of public speaking. For them, a small crowd is still a crowd.

Don't let your nervousness get the better of you. You, by nature, are a gifted storyteller with plenty of experiences and stories to share. It's an inborn skill that you've honed for the longest time possible. Now is the time to unleash that talent!

Asking For a Favor

You may be a little hesitant at first to try this, but this technique has helped thousands of introverts break out of their shell. Instead of relying on your natural (or non-existent) charm, you depend on the inherent kindness of other people to get the chance to know them.

It starts easily by approaching someone and asking them for a simple favor; nothing too big, of course. It just needs to be something that should only take minimum effort and a fraction of their time.

Think about asking them to hold your drink, or asking them if something is in between your teeth and the like. You can also ask them if your outfit looks fine or if there are creases on the back of your shirt.

After the favor, be sure to thank them and immediately initiate a conversation! You can start talking about why you had to ask them for that favor and the events that transpired during your day. Now that you've disarmed their defenses with your favor, it's easier to shift into a different topic to get their attention!

Positive Comments

Too afraid to ask for a favor? Afraid of getting rejected on the favor-asking level? You may want to try a simpler approach by just commenting on something that the other person has.

It's As Easy As Saying "Those Are Some Nice Shoes"

By beginning with a comment about the other person, you immediately shift the focus of the discussion onto them. This is good because people liked being talked about in a positive light. This also puts down their defenses and gives them a friendlier perspective of you.

It doesn't just work with shoes. You can comment on almost anything on the other person so long as you're not making fun of them. Here are a few other examples:

"I really like your shoes. Where did you get them?"

"That shirt really looks sharp. Where do you shop?"

"That bracelet is pretty. Is that from (insert name of the shop you know)?"

These are just a few examples. If you're really interested in someone, you'll pay attention to them and notice a few things along the way. When that happens, don't be afraid to talk to them about it. You might just learn something new from them.

Find Something In Common

This is where most friendships start. When you start listening to other people, don't just wait for the moment to start talking about yourself. Look for something you have in common with this person.

You might have shopped at the same place before. You might like the same music. You might share political views. You could have gone to an event before and you just didn't know each other.

When you find common ground, it's easier (not just for you) to feel comfortable around someone. Even if the point of your commonality is something mundane like reading the same newspaper, it's still a good anchor to strike up an even longer conversation.

Bring Gum

You may doubt the possibility of this working, but you have years and years of wisdom backing you on this bit of advice.

Everyone always complains that when they open a pack of gum, a swarm of people asking for gum will always follow. So, you dare not open a pack of gum with friends, unless you want to keep it all to yourself.

You may not believe this conclusion but bringing a pack of gum will provide you with an opportunity to break the ice with someone. Practices around the world can attest to that.

In some countries, when someone opens a pack of cigarettes for a quick fix, it's customary to offer a cigarette to someone who's near you out of politeness. It doesn't matter if you know them or not.

Apply the same line of thinking to gum. When you open a pack of gum in front of someone, you're more likely to offer them a stick if they aren't asking you for one. This provides you a chance to open a conversation!

On top of that, the gesture of offering gum lowers the defenses of the other person and places you in a positive light. All that for a stick of gum! You don't even have to be fussy with the type of gum you carry. You can go sugar-free if you're concerned about your sugar intake.

Signs of Rapport

Because communication is a two-way street, it's not just you that needs to get comfortable with someone. The feeling should be mutual. You can't have a rapport and a monopoly at the same time. A strong foundation of rapport has the following characteristics:

Mutual Concern – This is when you and the other party are looking out for each other. You both work towards the comfort of the other with your questions and statements.

Mutual Focus – You're both the focus of each other. When you're the one talking, your partner is genuinely concerned with what you need to say. It also goes vice-versa. When it's their turn to share something, they have your complete attention.

Synchronicity – This is when you share most of everything during your exchange. You have the same level of energy, tone of voice and general demeanor.

Most of the time, you won't notice these signs appearing in your encounters; especially when you're enjoying the conversation. The same thing can be said about the other party. You'll know if something is amiss when you don't feel the other party matching your mood and your behaviors.

When it comes to people in social interactions, many are grey mice. Some are darker or lighter grey - I really don't want to brainstorm about how many shades of grey there might be – but at the end of the day, they are hardly noticed.

How is it then that others can attract people like bees to honey?

These popular people can be anywhere, even buried in a soft couch, but you know their company is interesting, attractive, and that it makes you feel cooler even just to be in the same room with them.

And now that you look, you see someone else in the corner wearing grey, or brown… or whatever. Who cares?

Do you often feel like you're the one in the corner? The one nobody cares about? The one who came because you read about the event but weren't actually invited? Or did your crazy friend drag you to the party so she could see The Famous One only to ditch you in search of cooler people?

No matter which of these people you are, the result is the same. You are the one in the grey shirt, holding a paper cup of beer awkwardly and mildly shaking your head to the rhythm of the music to pretend like you're having fun.

On the outside, you seem… Chill? But inside, your head is full of chaos. All your brain cells are in emergency preparedness mode and on high alert to be able to answer questions like, "How do you do?" And, "What's your name?"

Odds are against you being asked a question that requires an answer of more than three words – including hi. And here comes that girl in the blue dress, she's approaching, very close...

She's Going To Talk To Me, What Should I Do??

Your inner alarm beeps loudly in your head, your heart rate rises to at least two thousand and clears the thoughts from your mind. You go completely blank. And suddenly... Miss Blue Dress changes direction and enters the restroom. You feel relieved and disappointed at the same time.

You feel relieved because you survived a certain social fiasco but disappointed because deep down you crave attention, some caring words, or just casual chit-chat or a connection. In reality, you would like to be like The Popular Person and to know what to say and when to say it. You'd like to be a natural connection-maker who never has sweaty palms.

Inside Out

First things first, you have to acknowledge that who you are on the inside will show on the outside. In other words, if you feel insecure, you have self-acceptance problems and a quitter attitude that will be clear to others. You don't like to be around this kind of person either, right?

I can't quit smoking. I've always been a smoker; I can't do it. I've always been a quitter. I am bad at conversations; I can't speak to people easily.

Familiar? Self-fulfilling prophecies. You know why? Because you believe them. I can't count on my fingers and toes how many of these iron-clad beliefs people construct and follow every day. I could also call them excuses, but whatever I call them, their impact is the same: they convince you that you are not good enough.

And in many cases, people create these excuses and negative beliefs in order to make others like them! They think people will feel sympathy for them.

Look at me, I am so bad at this, I can't do it on my own, I need help, please like me.

There is nothing wrong with having flaws, everybody has them, and indeed that makes us human. Our vulnerability is our armor but when it comes to social presence, people are more attracted to strength, powerful charisma, and a winning attitude. Even vulnerability is only attractive when it pairs up with courage. If you confess a weakness against your fears, the impact will come off as a demonstration of strength and gutsiness. For example, if you tell people that you often feel insecure about how to start a conversation, but you are doing your best to overcome it, many will sympathize with you, relate to your issue and admire you for being honest and open.

But if you talk about your weakness where you clearly search for external confirmation or denial, you complain and try to make all the conversation about you, that's not attractive. For example, you say something like, I know I am bad in starting conversations, or... is it really like this? Do you think I'm right? No? You think I'm good? No, you're just saying it to make me feel better. Or...? I don't believe it... Multiply this by ten and you get the topic of an entire evening in full.

So if you want people to like you, talking about your bad habits and weaknesses in a confirmation-searching manner won't help. At best, a few people will feel sorry for you. They probably are similar to you, and only listen so they can throw down their list of weaknesses later.

At the end of the day, nobody cares enough about you to think much about your words. People won't remember your words; they will remember how you made them feel. If they feel inspired and charged, they will want to connect with you more and slowly you will make your way into the center of the room. But if people feel drained by your constant complaining, they will avoid you.

In the worst cases, people will use your weaknesses against you, to mock or bully you. These are the social impacts of having a victim attitude.

How do you change them?

Opposite Searching Games

In this game, you claim the opposite of every negative self-label you ever think or say. So for example, if you say I'm a quitter, replace this by saying I'm a do-er. If you start a sentence with I am bad at... quickly correct it to I am good at.

If a defeatist, negative, or self-depreciating brainchild is coming to life in your head, quickly tell yourself STOP!!! STOP STOP STOP! And if it goes on the... STOP STOP! And still... STOP! But... STOP STOP!! Like this. Actually, if you say stop long enough you will forget completely about what your inner demon was even talking about. After stopping a negative feeling from conquering your brain, you can introduce a feeling of self-gratitude for chasing out the bad thought. Then just focus on your next task.

Let People like You for Who You Are

If you always say what you think others want to hear, you'll never feel true satisfaction in a conversation. You'll feel a strange gut-level squeeze because you know you didn't say what you wanted, and you won't achieve your goal of being more likable.

Find the Cause of Your Self-Destructive Thought

Is it because you lack self-confidence? Do you use forced incompetence as a coping mechanism? Or do you use self-pity as an excuse to stay inactive? Intentional self-harm in your self-deprecating words is a clear sign of self-hatred, which is mentally and physically damaging. You have to take serious actions to overcome self-destructive behavior.

Here are some quick tips on how to rethink what to say and not say to yourself:

Don't say something about yourself which you can't say about your mother, your lover, or your best friend. Every time when you feel that negative train coming, ask yourself: Would I say this about...? If your answer is no, then you don't deserve the bad label either.

Write it down: whenever you insult yourself, take a piece of paper, or your phone, and write down your self-deprecating remark. Seeing and reading it will reveal how absurd it sounds.

Stop Reading Beauty Magazines

Researchers have shown that regular readers of beauty magazines have a much higher level of self-criticism. First, acknowledge that the perfect men and women on the pages are Photoshopped. Then realize that those people cultivate their beauty for a living. They are not busy lawyers, tired nurses, or full-time stay-at-home mothers. Why read something that makes you feel ugly? Instead, see yourself as you are: a beautiful human being. Tell yourself something nice every day.

Those people who are ok with themselves have strong social charisma. They are balanced and in harmony with who they are. Social acceptance and respect does not come from beauty, but from an overall stable and reliable personality.

Why Do People Fear Social Interactions?

Am I good enough? I am sure she will do better on the evaluation because she is smarter, oh why can't I be like her? He is so good with words; everybody is hanging on to his every word. I will never attract that much attention.

Familiar thoughts? You can meet them at every corner of the road. But let's look at a comparison – who can invoke it and how can you handle it.

You are met with comparison from an early age. The most common ones that might affect you are those you get from your parents or close relatives.

- Why aren't you helping me more like Susan's daughter? Why aren't you studying as hard as your brother?

The example above is a very direct way of comparing, but there is another kind, the nasty, skin ripping kind that we also often meet.

- Oh, why do I deserve this? What have I done to earn such a never–does–well wife and dumbass kids? What will happen to the business if …?

In this sentence the subject of comparison wasn't mentioned–of course, it is the perfect dad for whom neither his wife nor his kids will ever be good enough. You may think these are everyday nothings, but I am telling you, they are serious offenses that stick. Growing up in an environment where you can never be good enough will leave such a deep conscious and/or unconscious imprint on your self-esteem that it will be almost impossible to leave it behind. This is a common and harmful underlying cause for a person's lack of social confidence. And it is the hardest to overcome.

Because even if you get over it on the surface, say you become fortunate and respected by society, when you go home and face that you are still not enough for your mother or not as good as your sister, those deep-rooted cramps erupt like a volcano and blindfold you, making you feel miserable and insignificant. Not enough. And your well-rehearsed mask instantly falls apart leaving you with the bitter feeling of inadequacy.

What can you do? Difficult question. Difficult because people's experiences in this regard are varied. The common thing is that they all have the same root: fear. Remember Yoda?

"Fear is the path to the dark side. Fear leads to anger. Anger leads to hate. Hate leads to suffering."

It is one of my favorite Star Wars quotes. You see, not only I think it is true, but also a Jedi master. And a Jedi master knows one or two things about human nature.

So what are people usually afraid of? The unknown. In your case, the undiscovered part is your soul, values, and skills. Here we go again—self-knowledge.

Do you believe you are worse than your brother or your workmate or that lingerie model from the poster? Honestly.

First, be aware of your values. Further in this book, I will give tips on how can you do that and how can you use self-knowledge to improve your relationship with others. The goal is to become 100 percent objective with yourself. After you feel you are okay, look objectively at your critics.

Are they a reliable model?

You know the universal truth: those who are positive about themselves don't criticize, they teach and inspire. So most probably your critics are people in a similar or even worse boat than you. And people who have spent enough time in the "shadows of lack of self-esteem" (maybe they faced similar problems as you did at their early age) tend to expand their acidity on those around them. Sometimes they are not even conscious; they just do it because that's what they saw, or how they were treated before.

Objectively these people do not deserve your sadness to fuel their venom, even if we're speaking about someone you love. If you think it over, you realize there is no point in you getting upset because the whole story isn't about you. It is about them. Their fears, rage, and inability to handle their past.

And believe me. As soon as you have a stable and objective picture of yourself, these shadows of the past will vanish.

But if after a profound and accurate self-evaluation, you still feel that even though they are not a valid model, they are right in certain situations, accept it. Not because they said so, or because you want to match their expectations, but because YOU realize that YOU indeed have an issue here that is disturbing for YOU.

Find the reason that you feel your brother, for example, is handling laziness, anger or stress better than you. Then find the connecting points— where and how can you improve yourself based on what you see from your brother?

Don't forget, every flaw can be reversed and be used positively for your benefit! You just realized and accepted that somebody is better than you at something, and instead of envy and fear, you decided to grow.

You just defeated one of your biggest demons! You used the power of comparison in a positive way, and you created an area where you can grow personally. This discovery can help you become less fearful when it comes to engaging with others. Make comparison your ally, not your enemy.

Ego vs. Self-Esteem

This is one of my favorite questions in regard to human existence. What leads us? What pushes us forward? Ego or self-esteem? First, I'd like to make my point with an illustrative comparison.

John's colleague tells him that his product design won't win the competition because he is not creative enough and he works too slowly. He'd better quit now.

John's ego's answer: How dare you?! I am good! I have a prodigious creative mind! Or maybe not, but now I will show you!! Scandalous! Who do you think you are? Oh, I will so show him!! I will prove him wrong even if it is the last thing I do, yes! – John thinks after his severe outbreak.

John's self-esteem answers: - Hm, funny guy. He didn't even apply for the competition. I did because I know I am good. And I trust my product. It fits the company's needs perfectly. So where was I? Ah, I know, I wanted a snack...

Ego gets angry and wants to show off – ME, ME, ME. Basically, this is the only thing it says. People with an overgrown ego seem very stark, and determined but deep down, they are full of fear and lack confidence. Just like in my example, the ego is focused on proving the colleague wrong. Why? Because John himself doesn't believe that he will succeed.

Meanwhile, John, with a strong self-esteem, stays calm. He knows he is able, that's why he entered the competition. He recognizes the envy behind his colleague's words, and he respects himself enough to not care about it. He knows his value, but he doesn't feel the need to brag or defend himself.

The strength of character comes with awareness; grit comes from the action that follows awareness. Otherwise, this whole thing is just a minute of vision for a blind man. He was ok, blind all along, but after seeing that one minute, he will be tormented and feel the sense of loss. He knows how different life could be. So why trade peace of mind for one lucid moment when he knows he won't change?

How do you usually react to criticism? Do you get angry and want to prove others wrong? Or you stay unaffected because you are perfectly aware of your virtues and flaws? In other words, does your ego or your self-esteem reply? If the former, make it shut up by developing a strong self-esteem. How?

Crush Emotional Spasms

What generates these spasms? Some people are scared to show their true selves because they fear rejection. So they put on masks and pretend to be strong, self-assured, and confident when in reality, they aren't. Behind these spasms – or we could call it ego - there is low self-esteem and a profound hunger for love.

How does a person without spasms act? This person is quick to smile (not a tormented grin but a sincere, heartfelt smile), laid-back, and spontaneous. People like this can straighten their backs; they believe in themselves. But there is hard work behind it.

How do you get rid of these spasms? First, you have to say this out loud:

I Have Spasms or I Have Trouble with This and That

Speak about it. It's a general misconception that if you talk about your problems you're weak. Some think strength means silently carrying the burdens but this is self-deception. I do not recommend it. However, even if you don't speak about it, spasms influence your charisma. They speak loudly even when you don't say a word.

To overcome a fear, you have to find words for them and say them out loud. If you don't speak about them in an effort to satisfy others expectations, you won't help yourself. Admitting your fears and weaknesses is a sign of strength. If you admit one, you'll get rid of one spasm. However, if you admit one but don't change it, your problems will only deepen. So admit it – say it out loud – and change it.

Learn To Be Humble

Ego and humbleness can't live together. On the other hand, self-esteem and humbleness walk hand in hand. If you know you are good at something, this is an amazingly healthy condition. Repeat your strengths to yourself as many times as you want. I'm a good mother, lawyer, writer, basketball player. This is perfect. Boost your mood and performance with this strong belief. If you are good at something why wouldn't you be proud of it?

Problems start when you start saying anthems about your skills to others without being asked. Then it becomes bragging and self-justification. It can also be a sign of compensation for an inner insecurity with a defensive action.

If someone accepts that you are a good designer, let's say, will your self-appraisal make you a better designer? Right? What if someone thinks you are a bad designer? You won't change their mind by telling that you're good. So why bother? Just be the good designer you are and your critic will see your results eventually.

The only time when it is not boastful or defensive to share your excellence in conversation is when someone asks. Then say:

Yes, I'm good at layout design. What about you? What's your superpower?

By telling the plain truth about yourself then quickly turning the focus back to the other person, you give the impression you are straightforward and curious. Your conversation partner will be happy to get to talk about him/herself – people love that.

False modesty gets an F.

False modesty, like boasting, is unlikeable. It is a passive way of bragging and can be displeasing. Remember the nerds of the class in school? When you asked them how the test was and they replied how awful then got the best score? So when you feel inclined to be falsely modest, just think about the nerds of your class. Also, false modesty is a form of insecurity – you just don't know how to receive compliments.

So instead of just sniggering awkwardly and denying the person's praise, just respond with a "counter compliment." Let's say somebody said you were a great designer. You reply:

Thanks, you have a sharp eye for quality.

This way you didn't deny your skills and you didn't seem over-confident either, like I know, right?

Shut down your ego and grow your self-esteem. Do it to balance your self-confidence, for peace of mind, and for unshakable persistence towards whatever you want.

Get Out Of Your (Un)Sociable Comfort Zone

Isn't it just easier to think when you approach something new that it won't work out so why bother trying? Did you already decide that you won't be welcome in certain company so you don't even make yourself known? Would you rather keep headphones in your ears to avoid people and conversations? And while listening to music, are you daydreaming about being the soul of a community (it doesn't matter if that community is a squad of cheerleaders, the chemistry club, a religious group, or a League of Legends faction)?

I bet you picture yourself being a great singer who is loved by many, living in another age, being super-successful and professionally admired, or being in a romantic relationship with Henry Cavill. Oh yeah... Ok, time to step out of fantasy world.

Good news, to some extent all of these dreams can be achieved, but not by staying motionless.

Being antisocial, in addition to dooming you to a lonely life, is physically unhealthy. According to research, loneliness can lead to several health diseases like stroke, depression, even suicide. So let's find the root of your antisocial behavior and cure it.

List Your Positive Qualities

To stop this way of thinking, make a list of your positive qualities. Include both emotional and physical characteristics. After making the list, remind yourself every day of these positive attributes. When a negative thought comes to mind, replace it with two positive ones.

Stop Labeling Yourself as Shy or Antisocial

I already mentioned this once but I'll say it again. The more you have negative thoughts about yourself, the more you will reinforce this belief! So if you constantly tell yourself you can't make social connections, guess what? You won't. But remember, all this mess is in your head so it only depends on you. If you want to be more social, start by actually believing you can be.

Take Action

"Do one thing every day that scares you." That's actually Eleanor Roosevelt's advice to you. In your case, this thing might be as simple as taking out your headphones. Listen to the sounds of nature, or to what people are talking about. It can be really interesting and you'll realize that it's not that difficult to hold a casual conversation.

When you're comfortable enough being without headphones, take this exercise to the next level. Go and talk to people. Start with an innocent excuse like asking the time or for directions. When you are confident enough, try to get somebody's phone number or connect with them on Facebook. Whatever it is, just be uncomfortable. That's not a typo. Get out of the comfort zone of your unsocial habits! Don't be pushy or harass anyone, just be friendly when the situation allows it. Practice.

Believe that human nature is good. There are cartloads of bad people out there, but trust that you won't meet them. It is important to know and accept that humans can be kind and accepting creatures. Isn't that a more encouraging approach when trying to meet new people?

Stop Over-Analyzing Your Interactions

Over-thinking social interactions can happen to either gender - whatever gentlemen might say - and it is what hinders people from enjoying social situations. Although it's not easy, it is essential to break the habit of trying to predict what social engagements will be like before they happen. And of course, you must break the habit of over-analyzing them word for word once they are over.

Approach every conversation with a positive attitude rather than focusing on how you would embarrass yourself and what could go wrong. Focus on the things that went well when the interaction is over instead of starting your analysis paralysis. Find a funny moment, new information you learned, or a thoughtful idea even if the interaction itself wasn't that earth shaking.

Just like any other skill, improving your social skills requires practice and persistence. It means you will have to get off the couch, get out of your comfort zone, and interact with people on a regular basis. After a while, it won't be a matter of demand, but a natural part of your day. There won't be "your life" and "your social life" parts of your day, but just a constant flow of natural interactions and time of your own. So if you are dedicated enough to becoming a social being, you will have to be social in all areas of your life regardless of if you are at work or school or simply at your family's dinner table.

People are exciting and so are you.

Don't Overdo It

Have you ever met somebody that was overly smarmy, trying too hard to please others? Like:

- What's your favorite color? – You ask.

- Blue. –Replies the pleaser.

- Oh cool, mine is green.

- Yeah, mine too.

And you feel like, what? I thought you said blue just a moment ago. Ok, this is a simplistic example, but you get the idea. This is when somebody is overly compliant.

The other way of overdoing it is, at a party, to spend too much time being an expert in... everything. Like when you see a painting on the wall and express your admiration:

- What a lovely picture!

- That's an early impressionist French painting from the 1870s.

- How do you know that?

- I've been studying art forever. It's pretty basic information.

Ok, cool, weird. Maybe the guy is an expert indeed. But just the next moment you see a cute kitten.

- That's a Burman-Siamese mix, 6 weeks old. I've been working with cats for twenty years. How can't you see that?

At this point everything becomes clear. This person is an eagle-eyed observer, master critic, and polymath at the same time. Also, highly unlikable. But the day is far from over and Mr. or Miss Mastermind has only shot half their wad.

I'm not saying you should play dumb or be tacit even if you know an answer, but stop trying to please or impress others. Also don't show too much of your skills, knowledge, and charm in a short period of time unless you're at a job interview. Less is more when it comes to human communication.

Stuck In Shyness

If you are reading this book, then you know what shyness is. And you know what "social anxiety" is, even if you have never used that term.

You know that tight feeling in your throat and the thumping in your chest before it is your turn to speak in a group. You know that intense feeling of fear and dread before you are going to start a conversation with that attractive person. And you know that nagging worry in your mind that just will not stop: What do they think of me? Did I do that right? Could they tell I was nervous?

How about that tense feeling in your stomach when you are about to meet someone new? When you are in that horribly awkward moment after you have both exchanged names and are standing there looking at each other, waiting, hoping that you will be able to think of something to say. You frantically scramble for some question, some observation, something, anything to say, but all your mind gives you is: Oh my god, you don't have anything to say. What's wrong with you? Say something!

The silence in this moment is not the sweet, peaceful silence you experience when you wake up before dawn or go for a hike in the forest alone. No, this silence is painful, pregnant with expectation and loaded with pressure. It feels like your skin is crawling, and you begin hoping one of the chandeliers will fall from the ceiling so you can make an unnoticed and hasty escape.

Can you relate? When was the last time you experienced something like this? If you are anxious around people, then you might have this experience all too often. In fact, this might be your primary experience of meeting people. You might have experienced this so often that you say things like:

I don't like going to parties.

I hate meeting new people.

I hate small talk.

People, they are so boring and only talk about stupid things that don't matter.

I'm so awkward.

I don't have anything interesting to say.

No one would want to talk with me when they could be talking to someone better.

I can't do that, I have social anxiety.

Uncovering the Roots of Your Social Anxiety

Do you want to find out what has been causing your social anxiety? If you do, then you will need a sheet of paper, a pen, a quiet place where no one would disturb you for a while, and maybe a cup of hot tea for comfort.

First, ask yourself, what could be the cause of your problems with social anxiety? Begin with your family. Do you have any relatives who may have or have had social anxiety?

It cannot be helped that genes play a role in the development of an anxiety disorder, although it should not be considered as the only factor. Social anxiety, for one, is typically triggered by an experience in the environment and most especially among peers. If you do have family members with an anxiety disorder, it is highly advised that you consult a health professional regarding the symptoms you are experiencing with relation to your anxiety.

The next thing to consider is whether your parents, guardians or other family members had influenced you to become socially anxious, whether it is them modeling the behaviors or having a parenting style that encourages –knowingly or unknowingly– such behavior.

While this should not lead to anyone blaming their parents for their social anxiety, reflecting on the kind of home environment you had as a child can help you uncover the reason behind your fears. It is important to remember, however, that parenting is one of the most difficult and challenging lifelong tasks because there is no perfect way to raise children with different personalities.

That said, children might grow up to have social anxiety if they are raised in a home where the parents overprotected them, controlled them too much, or were erratic in their parenting style.

Overprotective parents, for instance, would cause their child to be less exposed to frustrations, the feeling of being anxious or afraid, or failure. This will make such life experiences even more daunting to them for they have not been given the opportunity to overcome them in the past.

Controlling parents, on the other hand, do not foster independence and in fact, would instill constant anxiety in their children due to their rules and standards. Many children who grew up in this environment tend to become either rebellious or too dependent on others.

On the other hand, parents with unpredictable parental behavior are the ones who would be kind and loving one day, and angry and violent the next. Children raised in this erratic parenting style have the tendency to develop a lack of trust towards other people in general. They are also likely to develop anxiety because they feel as if they do not have any control over their lives.

With all this in mind, would you say that your home environment as a child played a role in your social anxiety? If you think that none of these would describe your situation, then perhaps we can look into the third set of factors, which is the environment beyond the home.

Negative Social Situations In the age of information and the internet, the world has become even smaller than before. Likewise, we have become even busier, filling our days with tons of task regardless of whether many of them are truly beneficial to our well-being or not. Therefore, it has become increasingly common for people to feel so stressed out that they become anxious in many given situations.

Many experts who study anxiety have identified three specific situations that can lead to the fear of certain social situations. Let us talk more about them so that you can determine which one has contributed the most to your social anxiety: An event in which one becomes the subject of uncalled for rejections, judgment, and/or criticism by peers is perhaps the most common social situation that triggers social anxiety. Even the most confident person in the world becomes vulnerable to self-doubt and constant worry over one's appearance, skills, talents, social background, et cetera, if their confidence is trampled by others.

For example, let us say you were unexpectedly invited to perform a song in front of a big party. You have always been confident with your voice and you have in fact won a few contests. However, in this unexpected situation, you were somehow unprepared and so halfway through the song; you forgot the rest of the lyrics. As the people laughed at and teased you for forgetting, you considered it such an embarrassment that you lost confidence in yourself.

The second anxiety-causing event is a traumatic experience, especially if it was a life-threatening or horrifying one. An act of terrorism, a natural disaster, violence, or a horrific accident could lead to severe anxiety problems.

Here is an example of how a traumatic experience could lead to social anxiety: let us say Bob was at a public speaking event when the main speaker was suddenly gunned down. The crowd turned into a raging stampede that left Bob severely injured and traumatized. Ever since then, he always avoided large crowds and any event where there is public speaking involved.

The third event is one in which a person has experienced an unforeseen threat, causing the person to lose a sense of security and stability. This may be regarded as a somewhat lighter experience as compared with a traumatic one, nevertheless, it is still quite damaging to one's sense of self-confidence.

For instance, let us say you used to be relatively well-off and could afford anything you wanted. You had many equally rich friends and you always attended major social gatherings together. Then, one day you lost all the money because you were unexpectedly laid off and ran out of what little savings you had. Because of this unforeseen circumstance, you begin to avoid any social situations with people who were with you when you still had money.

Which of these scenarios could you relate to the most? You do not have to delve deeply into the memory of that experience to know it was the one that caused your social anxiety. After all, that was in the past and no longer a part of your reality. What matters now is that you want to overcome your anxiety towards specific social situations. That way, you can enjoy a truly meaningful life.

Moving towards acceptance at this point, you probably already know what caused your social anxiety. If you still do not, then you might want to seek the help of a licensed therapist to help you uproot the underlying problem. However, if you can clearly state why you have social anxiety, then the next step is to accept that it is all in the past.

To help you with that, answer the following questions as honestly as you can. You may choose to write down your response or you can say it out loud to yourself. Here are the questions:

- Do I blame myself for my shyness?

- Do I purposefully want to be shy and anxious whenever I find myself in (a specific social situation)?

- If my best friend struggled with social anxiety, how can I help them?

- If I continue to worry and be fearful towards (a specific social situation), will my health, mood, and overall well-being improve?

- Am I capable of overcoming my social anxiety? What will happen if I do overcome it?

- If I could channel the energy I would normally spend on worrying and thinking negatively on something else, what would it be?

Take your time in answering these questions, especially when you notice that your mind tends to shift its focus back towards negative thoughts. If your negative thought patterns seem too overwhelming, however, then you will be able to progress well with the help of a mental health professional. He or she can guide you through the best therapy that will help you overcome social anxiety and your negative thought patterns.

Identifying the Intensity of your social anxiety if you tend to feel anxious towards a variety of social situations, and if you are not sure of where to begin in terms of overcoming your social anxiety, then it is best to have a professional conduct a clinical interview to help you specify your problem. To help prepare you for this interview, this section provides you with some of the commonly-asked questions. Try to answer them on your own using the following intensity scale

Limited Options, Limited Satisfaction

If you've been dealing with shyness for a while, then your choices regarding whom you talk to, what you can say, where you can go, and what you can do feel pretty limited. If your experience of meeting new people is frequently one of discomfort, awkwardness, and embarrassment, then most likely you avoid putting yourself in that situation. If you hate going to bars or parties, then you naturally do not go to those either. How do you deal with this?

The first step to breaking through shyness and social fears is to become more aware of what your fears are and how you respond to them. This awareness is the first step to shifting your patterns.

Remember the scenario described earlier where you are meeting someone new and you have nothing to say? If we were to turn that situation into a multiple-choice question, what would your options be?

You have just met someone new and exchanged names. You are both standing there looking at each other. No one has said anything yet. What do you do?

a. Blurt out a random comment, such as "Boy, it's sure been raining a lot, huh?"

b. Stare wide-eyed at the other person until they say something.

c. Wait for their lead, then nod and agree with what they are saying.

d. Give an excuse and exit the situation.

These are the most common options that we choose from when we are feeling anxious around others. None of these options are particularly satisfying. In fact, not only are they unfulfilling socially, each one actually has a downside that makes you feel worse afterwards. The next part of this book will help you see that you have much more satisfying options, and help you develop the courage and self-confidence to choose them. In the meantime, what option do you typically choose? What is your default?

Each response is worth examining briefly. Doing so will highlight the fact that none of them will give you what you truly want when connecting with others. As this becomes clearer, you will be able to learn new patterns that will increase your enjoyment of meeting new people and being around others.

Option A: "Sure been raining a lot, huh?"

Blurting something out can sometimes get the ball rolling in the conversation. In fact, turning down your filter and blurting things out can actually help your social life. However, saying something you are not really interested in—just to say something, anything—is the problem. This kind of comment is hard to respond to and often does not spark an interesting conversation. This can then kick your mind into an even higher gear: What the hell was that? Sure been raining a lot? Idiot! You're so awkward. What the hell is wrong with you? She thinks you're a freak. Look at you just standing there.

Now you are not only trying to start a conversation with someone you do not know, you are attacking yourself in your head. This can be incredibly distracting, can make thinking of something to say even harder, and can make you feel terrible about yourself.

Option B—Stare wide-eyed and wait

This option is not much better than A. For one, while you are waiting there, your mind can launch wave after wave of distracting and painful self-attack. Even when the other person does say something, you might be too distracted by your inner critic to respond effectively. Once your mind starts to become self-conscious and self-critical, it can be very challenging to remain present and spontaneous in a conversation.

Option C—Nod and agree with everything they say

Once the conversation is going, most shy people will choose option C. This involves being very agreeable, nice, friendly, and non-offensive. You nod as they are speaking, laugh at their jokes, and are sure to say things that you know they will like. Most shy people are highly intuitive and socially aware, so you are most likely able to guess accurately what the person wants to hear.

This was my default option for many years, and I notice I still fall back into this pattern when I am feeling nervous around someone. When you do not really like yourself, you tend to modify your behavior to get the approval you need from others.

At this point you might be thinking: Well what's wrong with option C? Isn't it good to be friendly, ask them questions about themselves, and avoid offensive topics?

In response to those questions, I have a question for you. How do you feel after an interaction like that? Are you satisfied, happy, fulfilled? Do you feel connected to that person and energized? Or do you feel uncomfortable, nervous, irritated or sad? Were you really interested in the conversation, or were you bored? Do you feel fulfilled and eager to connect with that person again, or do you feel tired and drained? Do you dread having more social interactions?

Many shy people I work with experience these feelings after being sociable. And many of them are choosing option C when interacting with others. While being warm, interested, and friendly are fantastic ways to connect with others, when feeling shy we often do this out of fear rather than genuine interest. We are also scared to share too much about ourselves, making the interaction one-sided and ultimately unfulfilling.

If you see yourself in option C, congratulations! Gaining awareness is an absolutely essential step in creating lasting change. In the next section, you will learn exactly why you choose option C again and again, even though it might not be completely satisfying. Then you will learn how to shift out of this pattern and into one that leaves you feeling happy and excited after social interactions.

Option D—Give an excuse and exit

This option is possibly the most common default, along with playing nice, nodding, and being overly friendly. In fact, when feeling social anxiety, many of us will go one step further and actually avoid the interaction entirely. This allows you to side-step the pain and embarrassment of that awkward conversation.

When we are feeling shy or anxious around people, it is very easy to develop many layers of avoidance. While this provides an immediate relief in the short term, it can actually worsen shyness over time and can leave you feeling unfulfilled and lonely. One level of avoidance is to immediately end the conversation as quickly as possible. Many people I work with say they often do this when speaking with someone they find attractive.

Shy Quote:

I don't know why I keep doing this, but as soon as a woman I'm interested in starts talking to me, I have a strong desire to flee the situation. I become tense, cold, and unresponsive and just keep looking for a way out. Then afterwards I beat myself up for not being more confident.

Noticing your desire to avoid the uncomfortable situations is a key step in breaking the patterns of shyness. The primary pathway to a life of lasting confidence and trust in yourself is to steadily and regularly step outside of your "comfort zone." This involves doing things that you used to avoid and approaching what scares you in social interactions. At first, this might feel incredibly uncomfortable, like jumping off the high dive at a pool. However, over time you will start to see that you get accustomed to trying new things and that what once scared you no longer seems so intimidating.

Before embarking on that journey, however, it is essential that you have a clear understanding of why you would choose any of these unfulfilling options in the first place. All of these choices are the result of feeling afraid and anxious during a social interaction.

Reading Other People

Of course, how can you muster all previously discussed skills and call yourself confident if you can't manage to read other people?

Considered by some people as skills meant for con-men and criminals, the skill of reading people isn't just something people use to trick others. You can also use this skill to create better relationships and establish yourself as someone trustworthy.

Is Reading Possible?

On a certain level, anyone can be taught to infer from verbal and nonverbal cues given off by a certain person. In fact, this is rudimentary training for anyone working in the FBI and NBI and any other intelligence-oriented company and agency.

This chapter will give you an insight as to what it's like to read people and how you can apply these principles into your daily encounters.

The first and only thing you will need is a keen mind and an open eye. Where will you base your theories if you fail to notice anything? The best readers in the world don't just take note of the color of your shirt. They'll probably also check the brand and fabric if they could.

It's not only those details that you need to look out for. What sorts of mannerisms can you see in this person? Do they scratch their heads or rest their fingers on their temples? When do they do these things?

There are also verbal cues such as their word choice and tone of voice. Do their sentences treble at certain points? Is their vocabulary wide and do they use a lot of multisyllabic words to confuse others? Noticing these details will make it easier to make guesses as to what goes on in someone else's mind.

Placing Things into Context

Before you start watching someone like a hawk, you should put things into proper perspective. When you notice something aggressive like a crossing of the arms, it would be unwise to think that the person is looking down on you. It could just be because the room is cold and they don't have a jacket on them. This is also known as the test of common sense.

Before making the wrong assumption, try to ask yourself, is this person supposed to behave in this manner given the environment? This person's behavior may not be because of you. It could just have been because of your area. Is this person scratching his throat out of frustration and distaste for you? Or is it because he's just thirsty?

Setting a Baseline

What's worse than taking things out of context? Failure to establish a baseline for someone, that's what. A baseline is a set of values and behaviors which you consider to be "normal" for a certain person. If someone always speaks in a loud voice because they're naturally loud, that doesn't really give you information.

This person's loudness is your baseline. If they are behaving in such a manner, then that means they're okay and nothing is bothering them. On the other hand, if this usually loud person suddenly tones down and lowers their volume, then you know that something is amiss with this person.

Without a proper baseline, you're unable to tell which behaviors and cues are out of the ordinary. Think of it as your point of reference regarding this person. You may have already established baselines with your friends because you know them already. Isn't it easy for you to tell if there's something bothering them? That's because you can tell that their current behavior is unlike their baseline.

Watch Your Bias

When you've already made up your mind about someone, reading them becomes harder. This is because you now include a personal bias in your observations. It doesn't matter whether you like or dislike a certain person. These feelings of yours do not contribute to the integrity of the information you're reading from the other person.

Try to leave your personal feelings out of the way when you need to get a read on someone. Your feelings, along with the context and your baseline, will form a steady foundation of first-hand knowledge of someone. When you've got those three lined up already, you can now begin considering someone else's actions.

Reading Body Language

Now that you're ready to look deeper at a person's behavior, it's time to look at some simple cues that will tell you a lot about how one person feels when you open your mouth.

Crossing

Whether it's the arms or the legs, this signifies a certain amount of resistance to your content. When people feel uncomfortable with an idea or a statement, their tendency is to "defend" themselves from these things. This need to defend is manifested in the crossing of their arms or legs.

In a way, it signifies them not being open to what you're giving. Regardless of their facial expressions and the tone of their voice, if they're crossing something, it probably means what you said didn't sit well with them.

Smiles

It was mentioned in an earlier chapter that it's important to smile because it says a lot about your disposition and how approachable you are. Despite that, smiles can be faked as well. Someone may seem happy to be with you, but could just be screening their true feelings.

So, look straight into the eyes of someone who smiles. A real, genuine grin makes its way to the eyes, causing their corners to "crinkle". That results in what most people call "crow's feet" around those corners. If the feet aren't there, then that smile is probably forced and there's a different story behind that smile.

Space

Have you ever fantasized about being in a position of power? Have you ever had thoughts that you were the owner of your own successful company that had a following of loyal people? How about a very charismatic leader with plenty of believers?

When you feel like you're in a position of power, your brain tells you to take up more space than usual. This behavior can manifest itself in several ways. You could be taking longer strides. You could also be sitting with your legs wide apart. You also tend to make big hand gestures that require more elbow movement to take up more space.

If you notice these signs in someone, it gives them an aura of authority once they enter a room. Chances are, they do hold a certain authority. In other cases, this authority may not be implied and this person just really thinks highly of himself. Whatever the case, they feel that they have power in the situation.

Eye Contact

You've learned in the previous chapter that maintaining eye contact is a good way to establish trust and sincerity. Unfortunately, dishonest people have now adapted to this age-old wisdom by training themselves to look people in the eyes when they lie.

Fortunately, people who are hiding something take eye contact too far. Studies have shown that people that maintain more than 20 seconds of eye contact tend to be hiding something and they are attempting to convince you otherwise by compensating with eye contact.

Being stared at in the eyes for too long can make you feel uneasy as well as if someone was forcing you to maintain the contact. When you get that feeling, there's a good chance that the "sincere" glare you're getting is hiding a different story underneath.

Humor

Fancy yourself a comic genius? Are there certain people in your networks that make you laugh a lot? Is there one person you know who you'd like to invite over frequently because of all the funny things they tell you?

There's a large chance that person is very smart. Studies have shown that humor closely relates to intelligence. There's something about being funny that requires a bit of brainwork. This is where the adjective "witty" comes in.

If someone strikes you as funny, their brains are adept at finding the unusual in usual things and twisting them into amusing statements or stories for other people. That takes a good thinker. If you want to be liked by a lot of people, it's also a good idea to work on your punchlines.

Dealing with Rejection

Among all the skills mentioned in this book, this one may be the most helpful. You won't win them over every time; so, what do you do when that happens? What does that say about yourself as a person? What are your thoughts when someone doesn't allow you to reach out to them? What do you do when you're ignored?

The Fear of Rejection

Are these the things you think of even before approaching someone? Is your fear holding you back? Often, the fear of rejection and failure has prevented people from doing what they want. It's also the number one reason why shy people are afraid of social interaction.

When this fear sets in, it's usually because of several mindsets that may already be present in your life. Consider these mindsets and see if any of them correlate to the way you think.

Getting rejected is a painful experience.

It is your obligation to make everyone like you.

Your past rejections are proof that you can't take any more rejection moving forward.

Your failures are always going to stay in the back of your mind and you will always remember them.

You've had all the chances to make friends before. These opportunities are rare and you've squandered all your luck.

Do any of these statements describe the way you feel about rejection? If yes, then you simply have the wrong mindset. Take note that your fears should not stop you from trying.

The Wrong Mindset

People with low social confidence blame themselves when their plans go wrong. Because they like to examine themselves too much, it is likely that they'll conclude that they did something wrong, or worse, that something is wrong with them.

You may have experienced rejection before. Were those your thoughts? Did you think that it was something you said? Were you too forward? Was there something in your teeth?

These are the wrong thoughts to have after a rejection. After all, it could be anything. Have you ever thought that this person just wasn't in the mood to talk? They could have something important on their minds. They could have been worrying about something else. Unless you know the specific reason, brooding about it being your fault will not do anything for you.

The Right Mindset

It was the author Robert Greene in his famous "Art of Seduction" book that best encapsulates the right mindset.

Not everyone can be wooed. There will be times wherein your best efforts to reach out will come to nothing, and it won't always be your fault. Even the best and most charming people can fail to win over someone from time to time.

Try to think of your favorite band or actor. You probably have good reasons to idolize this person or group. When you talk about these people with other people, do they also tend to like them? Chances are, there will be someone that does not agree with you.

Take some age-old wisdom in this new-age set of problems: you can't make everyone happy. In the same way, you can't get everyone to like you. It shouldn't be your goal in the first place. When things go sour, the best thing you can do is to brush it off and move on.

Doing so may not be so easy, though. Just like suspending your personal beliefs to reach out, it takes some time to suspend your judgments of yourself when you get rejected.

Getting Over Rejection

This book isn't saying that rejection is nothing and that it shouldn't hurt. It does really hurt to get rejected. That much is true. This is because of an underlying connotation of a rejection: you're not good enough for someone's time.

You may not say that loudly, but you're thinking about it as you brood over your failure. That's not a welcome thought by anyone's standards. That's quite a painful thing to think about. In fact, the thought of rejection activates the same regions the brain activates when it goes through actual pain experienced through your senses.

It's painful. The worst part is that painkillers and a good night's sleep aren't enough to deal with the mental torture that is the aftermath of a rejection.

By instinct, you begin to doubt your worth and your capacities because you "seem" to have found empirical evidence that you're not good enough.

The Rug Approach

That "evidence" of your inadequacies may not be as solid as you think. One way to deal with this mindset is to take the rug approach.

Have you ever found yourself in a situation wherein your friend bought this rug for their house and asked your opinion of it? Your friend seems to think that it's a beautiful rug and spent a bit of money on it.

You, on the other hand, find the rug rather distasteful and are shocked that your friend spent good money on it. You do not like this rug at all.

Given your separate and different opinions of the rug, who do you think is right? Is it your friend that spent their own money on the rug? Or is it you that just gave your honest opinion?

In the end, it doesn't matter. The rug is still a rug, regardless of what you or your friend thinks.

The same line of thinking can be applied to your personal case. Rejection is not a qualitative report of your worth as a person. It's just someone's judgment of you. Regardless of that opinion, you are who you are.

It's a perception of you made by someone else. This person doesn't know a lot about you. Why should a negative perception made by someone who doesn't know you affect the way you see yourself?

Shift the Focus

Don't like comparing yourself to a nice rug? This just shows how well you can focus all your attention towards a single event. You can only see that kind of concentration in monks and sword swallowers.

What if you took that focus and placed it somewhere worthwhile? That one rejection may have been surrounded by others' successes that you have failed to see. When you get rejected, think about all the other times you could reach out to someone.

Don't look at the people that didn't give you a second look. Instead, focus on the things that you've already accomplished. Look at the friends that you already have. Look at the relationships you've already built with other people.

Draw from these positive events and you'll soon forget about your rejection as you take on the next opportunity that comes your way.

Self-Love
If you let the fear and pain of rejection get the best of you, then that probably means you don't think well of yourself. You would do well with a little self-approval.

How can other people like you if you don't even like yourself? One of the biggest tenets of social confidence is the belief in one's own self. It's wrong to draw confidence from that one time you sat down with someone you liked and got their number. Instead, draw confidence from the fact that you were brave enough to do that despite the possibility of being rejected.

At the end of the day, the only approval that matters should be that of your own. Once you start respecting and loving yourself, your self-worth will naturally come out and invite others to start seeing the good in you as well.

When this happens, you take away the power of your own fears and completely come out of your shell. What's not to like about you? You should be asking yourself how many things are there to like about you?

Conclusion

The combination of the skills you've covered in this book will improve your confidence. You don't draw each of those skills out individually to become confident, though. You tackle new encounters with all these principles in mind.

Now here comes the hard part: actual practice. These skills will only remain as studied material unless put to good use. This is where you need to get up on your feet and meet new people.

With that notion in mind, it's time to come out of your shell and step out of your comfort zone. Go ask a friend out for coffee or approach that other regular you see at the bookstore.

Applying the things you've learned in this book is going to take time, and you're bound to run into a few snags and rejections while you're practicing. Don't let these setbacks hold you back.

Take a lesson from almost every athlete in existence. The only way to sharpen and improve a skill or talent is to constantly use it. If you give up after a few tries, everything you've learned from this manual will go to waste and it'll just be another uplifting read that will collect dust.

Another good way to practice is to bring a friend with you. Trying new things is always more enjoyable in the company of friends. Take a fellow shy person and share this manual with them. You won't just be meeting new people, but you'll also be helping another individual realize their social confidence.

Finally, use the knowledge you've learned from this book to become a better example for other people. Don't just bask in the limelight once you've unleashed your confidence. Show other people that need pushing that they can do it too.

This can be done by reaching out to other people that don't seem to enjoy social gatherings. These are usually people that remind you of the person you were prior to reading this manual. By reaching out to these people, you're extending a helping hand to help someone else reach their true potential as a social creature.

If you enjoyed this book, please take the time to share your thoughts and post a review on Amazon. It would be greatly appreciated!

Printed in Great Britain
by Amazon